MW01533135

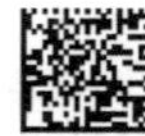

CPSIA information can be obtained
at www.ICGtesting.com
Printed in the USA
LVHW050918140120
643554LV00002B/225

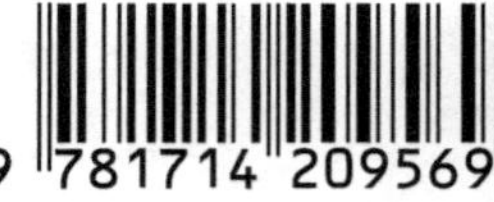